ECHOES
OF BROWN

**YOUTH DOCUMENTING AND PERFORMING
THE LEGACY OF BROWN v. BOARD OF EDUCATION**

Michelle Fine, Rosemarie A. Roberts, María Elena Torre

with

Janice Bloom, April Burns, Lori Chajet,

Monique Guishard and Yasser Arafat Payne

The Graduate Center, City University of New York

ECHOES OF BROWN v. BOARD OF EDUCATION

This 55-minute educational video captures youth and elders
in conversation about the history and legacy of Brown v. Board of Education.
Situated in the Art and Social Justice Institute, 13 students from diverse
backgrounds collaborate with artists, academics and elders, and explore original research,
history and personal experience. Together they have produced a
performance of dance and spoken word that addresses the (in)equities
and possibilities of schooling today in the United States.

INTERVIEWS WITH ELDERS

YOUTH SPOKEN WORD PERFORMANCES

BEHIND THE SCENES WITH ARTISTS AND EDUCATORS

**DOCUMENTING THE LEGACY OF BROWN:
RESEARCH FINDINGS FOR 2004**

**INTERVIEWS WITH RESEARCHERS ON
PARTICIPATORY WORK WITH YOUTH**

THE ART AND SOCIAL JUSTICE INSTITUTE

**INTERVIEWS WITH EDUCATORS ON THE RICHNESS
AND CHALLENGES OF DESEGREGATION**

CREDITS AND CONTACT INFORMATION

INSIDE THE BOOK

ECHOES OF BROWN

Linda Brown, 9 years old, stands in front of segregated
Monroe Elementary School, Topeka, Kansas, 1953.

Photo by Carl Iwasaki / Time Life Pictures / Getty Images

ECHOES OF

THE LEGACY OF BROW

**If you are neutral
in situations of injustice
you have chosen
the side of the oppressor.
If an elephant has its
foot on the tail of a mouse,
and you say that you are neutral,
the mouse will not
appreciate your neutrality.**

—

Bishop Desmond Tutu

Over the last nine months, we have gathered a collective of 13 youth—drawn from wealthy and economically depressed communities in the suburbs surrounding New York City and within the city; representing the kind of wisdom born in Advanced Placement classes and the kind born in Special Education classrooms. We joined Christians, Jews, Muslims and youth with no religious affiliation; those of European, African, Caribbean, Palestinian, Latino and blended ancestries; young people headed for the Ivy League and some who have spent time in juvenile facilities; some who enjoy two homes, and some who have spent nights without a home. Together we created a Social Justice and Arts Institute where we immersed ourselves in the history of the *Brown v. Board of Education* decision, in lectures, readings, music and discussion, as well as the findings of our own research with nearly 10,000 youth nationwide.

BROWN

BOARD OF EDUCATION FIFTY YEARS LATER

Simultaneously we interviewed elders who worked for civil rights during the 1940s through to the present day. Doubly-clothed, then, in the history of struggle and the evidence of contemporary (in)justice, we dipped into the inviting waters of spoken word, and moved to the rhythms of dance. In a scholarly and aesthetic experiment that challenges the boundaries of time, geography, generation and discipline, we braided political history, personal experience, research and knowledge gathered from a generation living in the long shadow of Brown, with performance. Stretched like the tight and yet elastic leather that protects and re-sounds percussion, across the generations of our research collective, we have produced *Echoes: The Legacy of Brown v. Board of Education, Fifty Years Later.*

This work grows from the rich soil of social discontent, from the vibrancy of social movements, from the wisdom of social research with and by youth about the state of racial, ethnic and class (in)justice in the nation. Anticipating the 50th anniversary of the Supreme Court decision on Brown v. Board of Education, three years ago we designed a participatory research project with high school students, **The Opportunity Gap Project**, to investigate the legacy of Brown, then and now. At that point, university researchers from The Graduate Center, City University of New York joined with public school educators, middle, high school and college youth to learn how young people think about racial justice in their schools and in our nation. Across suburban and urban districts, in New York, New Jersey, Delaware and California, we collected almost 10,000 surveys, conducted dozens of focus groups and individual interviews and visited each others' schools. We studied up on the history of Brown, Emmett Till, Ella Baker, Bayard Rustin, finance inequity, tracking, battles over buses and bilingualism, the unprecedented academic success of the small schools movement, new schools for lesbian/gay/bisexual/transgender students, the joys, the dangers and "not-yets" of integration. We read on the growth of the prison industrial complex at the expense of public education, and we reviewed how systematically federal policy has left so many poor and working class children behind. We wrote scholarly and popular articles, delivered professional and neighborhood talks. We traveled the nation to gather insights, listen to young people and to provoke policy, practice and change with our research. Learning well the lessons of the Brown strategy, we too joined social research and social struggle, for social justice.

But as we traveled with the stories of our findings, we worried about the limits of talk. We grew weary as we watched many cry, responsibility perhaps wiped away as tears. We saw most nod in solidarity, but met far too many adults who refused to listen to young people's complex renderings of Brown's victories and continuing struggles. We sat inside schools where it was clear that the "Achievement" Gap—the latest face of Segregation—was not so much about the youth as the politics, finances and (dis)respect surrounding them. We found ourselves trapped by obsessive questions pointing to poor youth and youth of color—*What's wrong with them? Even in the same school building, we have a gap? But if we stop tracking how else can we teach students at their "natural" levels?* Yet, at the same time, we found encouragement in our research with New York City's small inquiry-based schools, where recent immigrants and youth of both poverty and means, engage together in deep intellectual work, moving toward college, beating the odds.

And so, on the wings of Brown and the backs of social movements and activist performers who came before and after, we moved to a new genre of public scholarship blending social science, art and activism—to be in conversation and *movement* with a community of elders, youth, and those in between, to create, as Maxine Greene would urge, "A world [that] may come into being in the course of a continuing dialogue..." A world challenged by collective thought and action, diverse histories and passionate convictions across generations.

Echoes of Brown bridges 50 years of critique and hope, vision and disappointment. Through our work, we challenge the nation to rise to the promise of Brown, to resist the current assault on public education. We perform victory and dissent as the democratic exercise of respect and belief in Brown—then, and justice not—yet. We refuse to silence the troubles of realizing Brown, as if silence were a measure of loyalty. To the contrary, our collective desire for justice and democracy in education, our collective sense of betrayal and yearning, spoken and danced by white, black and brown bodies—together—has electrified the legacy of Brown, sustaining the vision of thousands who gave their lives for the struggle. Because we believe the Brown decision was so pivotal to the history of American education and democracy, we dare to speak about what has been, and what must be.

Together, in our small integrated research camps and institutes across the last three years, we've created intimate communities of young scholars, poets, dancers, activists, allies and witnesses, warmed by outrage and fueled by hope; reflecting back on struggles of yesterday, and looking forward toward tomorrow, demanding simply what Brown so boldly carved into our national conscience—democracy and justice for all. Awed by how far we have come, and bowed by how far we have to go, we give you *Echoes*. We ask that you bear witness with us, to a work borne of social research and social struggle, a work that blends history, politics and passion, stretched over the life of our nation, with flames burning still today. We ask you to be with us, for as James Baldwin wrote years ago, *"People who shut their eyes to reality simply invite their own destruction, and anyone who insists on remaining in a state of innocence long after that innocence is dead turns himself into a monster."* We ask that you listen to the echoes that reverberate between and among elders and youth, vibrations that join and separate across time, space, and bodies, bridging a social movement for social justice across differences—so that all young people can find spaces to learn, to stretch, to grow, to teach and be respected, surrounded and strengthened by the rich and varied humanity that sustains our nation.

—Michelle Fine, May 2004

ELDER INTERVIEWS

ARTHUR KINOY

(1920–2003) Professor of Law, Emeritus,
Rutgers University and co-founder of the Center
for Constitutional Rights.

"In the airport I was met by four Black ministers, fine people, and they took me to the only place where Whites and Blacks could meet, legally—the Black church. I walk in, and an older Black woman throws her arms around me, 'Arthur, they got five years in jail for marching down the street, a terrible evil thing they did, marching for the Constitution!' And then a young man named Martin says to me, 'Sir, with all due respect, tomorrow when you go in there, remind them that there are, in fact, four branches of government: the executive, the legislative, the judicial and The People. Please tell him you represent The People.' **And so I did; that turned out to be Martin Luther King**.

The next day I go down to the courtroom, and there are 200 or 300 African American people, all sitting in the back, the ones who had been arrested. And the judge says, 'Who are you?' And I say, because we had a little law firm in those days, Kunstler, Kunstler and Kinoy, 'I'm from the new KKK!' I'll never forget, everyone started applauding. And that night, we had a wonderful celebration in Mississippi. We were drinking and eating, when my friend, Fannie Lou Hamer, pours out a little bourbon, throws her arms around me, raises her glass and shouts, **'I want you to meet my People's Lawyer! Power to the People!'**"

August 8, 1963, Washington, D.C., Leaders of the March on Washington lock arms and put hands together as they move along Constitution Avenue. The Rev. Martin Luther King, Jr., is in the center. © Bettmann/CORBIS

SONIA SANCHEZ

Poet, professor of English and Women's studies, Emeritus, Temple University.

"And so to the young people I say, resist.

I wrote a poem for
Sweet Honey in the Rock that begins...

'I'm gonna stay on the battlefield until I die...
come. I say come, you sitting still in domestic bacteria
come. I say come, you standing still in double-breasted mornings
come. I say come, and return to the fight.
This fight for the earth
This fight for our children
This fight for our life
We need your hurricane voices
We need your sacred hands
I say come, sister, brother to the battlefield
Come into the rain forests
Come into the hood
Come into the barrio
Come into the schools
Come into the abortion clinics
Come into the prisons
Come and caress our spines
I say come, wrap your feet around justice
I say come, wrap your tongues around truth
I say come, wrap your hands with deeds and prayer
You brown ones
You yellow ones
You black ones
You gay ones
You white ones
You lesbian ones
Comecomecomecomecome to this battlefield
Called life, called life, called life....'"

ESTHER LEE

Executive Director, Jersey City
Child Development Centers, retired.

"In that sense, Brown v. Board of Education had a profound effect in organizing and mobilizing African Americans in the South, and also in the North. **The ripples of Brown created the leadership and organizing that shaped the future of this country.**

In South Carolina, 1954, the superintendent of a school district, interviewed me and offered me a job. I signed a contract. But a few days later I got a call at home. He said that he had two questions that he neglected to ask me, and asked that I meet him at the corner of Broad Street, I'll never forget, by the Liggett Pharmacy.

So I got there, and he said, 'I have two simple questions for you. First, how do you feel about the Supreme Court decision, and second, have you ever been a member of the NAACP?'

I knew this job was gone. I responded, 'Well, sir, I've been a member and am a member of the NAACP, and as for the Supreme Court, it should have happened a long time ago.'

He smiled a smile I'll never forget and said, 'Well, m'am, you have a right to your opinion, but I can't have you influencing my teachers.'

I lost that job."

"The Brown case was a pivotal decision in race matters in this country. In the 1930s it was the anti-lynching legislation that was the crucible for Congress people. But with World War II, because of the success of the Tuskegee Airmen, the Triple Nickel and the U.S.S. Mason, we had President Truman's Executive Order 9181, in 1948, desegregating the Armed Forces, then Jackie Robinson in 1947, and others too. The movement against segregation catalyzed in the Brown decision, nine for and none against. Between Tuskegee and Jackie, you might say that the mass of Whites got to see our contributions.

But it took 16 years before integrated schools would become a reality. George Wallace stood on those steps and said, 'Over my dead body.' And he lived to be asking for Black support.

I like to say that I first became an American citizen on May 17, 1954 when the umbrella of separate and equal was removed. But as far as we've gone, we've got a long way to go. As Frederick Douglass wrote, **'Power concedes nothing without pressure.' So I say to young people, 'Agitate, agitate, agitate. Stand up for what you believe.'"**

ROSCOE BROWN, JR.

Director, Center for Urban Education Policy, The Graduate Center, CUNY.

JUDGE JACK WEINSTEIN

Senior United States District Judge,
Eastern District of New York.

"The Brown case was a revelation. In order to understand the emotional impact of Brown, I have to go back to World War II. The Nazis were killing millions of people deliberately by denigrating them, telling them they were worthless. Once people accept that, they could be destroyed, they could be killed. We, in this country, had been discriminating against African Americans, obviously during slavery but also post-slavery, so both I and the people in the country generally had to face this at home. **After World War II, it was like a mirror we had to face. We were fighting the Nazis, but look what we are doing here in this country.**

So many of my religion were killed in Europe. I could no longer ignore what discrimination meant on a massive level. I had to face up to what discrimination meant in the U.S., [so that's when I decided I needed to go South and begin] working with Thurgood Marshall. I could no longer ignore the costs and unfairness we endured in this country.

The Brown decision was an inevitable decision because the U.S. could no longer exist half free and half unfree. **The world could no longer go on that way.**"

ADAM GREEN

Assistant Professor of History and
American Studies, New York University.

"[I would tell young people] History is not a church that you go into, fall silent, bow and show reverence. **The past is something you have a dialogue with, a conversation. The past is something you shape.** It will be different based on what you do with it. You can have a profound effect on history. In twenty years you will be the custodian of history. With any history, but especially African American, it is an opportunity and a burden to carry history, to change it. That's where the potential to effect change comes from.

You have to learn that just because you get a piece you can not be comfortable. Look at the breaks you got, look at who still suffers. The kind of integration people struggled for has not been achieved; maybe the kind of integration the Supreme Court was imagining—access for those who would be just like them—maybe that has been achieved. But that's not real integration. **The fight now is whether or not people can be seen for who they are, and who they can be, not to be seen by teachers, or police or shop keepers, as someone else thinks they should be.**"

THEA JACKSON

Former Deputy Director of the New York State Office
for the Aging, and advocate for prisoner education.

"It is to no one's advantage to become a melting pot, to become one. **When we work for sameness, we all lose.** There's still a great deal to do. If all of the apples in the world get colored red, we lose a great deal.

The majority of Blacks are still subjected to substandard education. It's not insignificant that most prisoners come from poor Black and Latino neighborhoods with substandard education."

BAILEY JACKSON

Retired optomechanical engineer who
worked on the Hubble Space Telescope.
Currently an advocate for prison education.

"There's a song, 'If ever you get a chance to dance,
dance.' I was thinking how expensive it is for one
group of people to hold back another group, White or
Black. **You can't dance if you have one foot on someone else's neck. This society of ours has got to
dance. We have got to dance. We have to recognize
that every man is my brother, White, Black, Red or
Yellow.** I think when we reach that point, we can
dance. ...I think we'll get there. I think I can hear them
striking up the band."

Free Your Mind
and your sorry ass
will follow

What is the meaning of C.L.A.S.
Conspiracy levelled at sleepy students
trying to pass.

－MCPB

Dean HAS Change
404 to be Exact.

Inspire
the mind
that sorrows
YOU!

[2637] PEOPLE LAUGHING AT WHAT YOU THINK,
UPPER CLASS PICKING ON YOUNGER STUDENTS,
AND A LOT OF RACISM

Tracking
Sucks!

I also don't understand
Why school funds are always cut
First! Can We all Make an Effort
to change this Education System!

Colombiano
y
Dominicano
PA QUE LO SEP

THE WORST POSSIBLE

SCHOOL EXPERIENCE:

Open to
beautiful—to know

REVOLUTIC

[2575] ISOLATION AND A FEELING OF STUPIDITY

[755] BEING COMPLETELY BORED IN THE
CLASSROOM HAVING NO OPPORTUNITY TO SEE MY
FRIENDS AND NOT HAVING A RACIALLY DIVERSE
ENVIRONMENT IN WHICH I CAN LEARN

to trust RAB

Who Farted?

[2478] BEING ALONE AND DONT SPEAK THE SAME
LANGUAGE AS EVERYBODY ELSE

Revolution
is
MY WAY
of life

[3540] I FEAR THAT ONE DAY I WILL DROP OUT OF
SCHOOL B/C OF STUPIDITY OR SOMETHING ELSE

genetic peatree dish
...pisstree dish

See yourself
through
my eyes

What is my class
sification?

I forge
Chocola
B/C
(I still

both at me and think, hmm
a couple noodles short of
a casserole

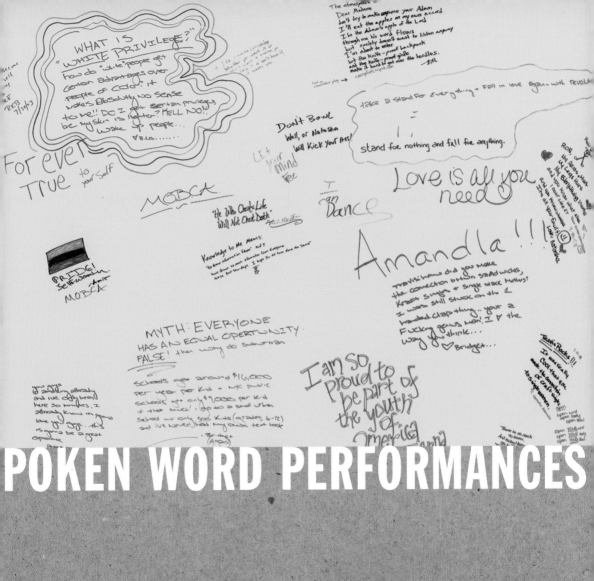

POKEN WORD PERFORMANCES

OF OUR FUTURE

by Tahani Salah

I found your eyes hidden I'm mind boggling
black outs never understanding where they
began or ended or where to pick up and start over.
I WON'T LET YOU RUN THROUGH ME like you've done
the souls and minds of my loved ones leaving

X MARKED SCARS AND HEART ACHE MILES LONG.

You forever trying to leave my soul reaching
levels of anger and anguish.
NO! No more. Picture this lion's den, you
cornered, no escape.

YOU'VE PICKED THE WRONG BATTLE

THE WRONG FIGHT
THE WRONG WAR

NAME Tahani Salah

AGE 17

SCHOOL Brooklyn School for Global Studies, Brooklyn, NY.

Hopes to study English in college, attend law school & become an international business lawyer.

I have found you with self inflicted wounds
and damaged {conscience} don't shore on spelling of this word
I AM JUSTICE STANDING ON MOUNTAIN TOPS screaming releasing me
I am holding lemons to make **FUTURE LEMONADE** in one hand and
life's decisions in another.

DIVERSITY IS OUR BEAUTY AND INTEGRATION OUR BLOOD

as it flows down the roads that we walk on screaming,

THE PEOPLE UNITED SHALL NEVER BE DEFEATED.

With reason centuries old

IT IS NOW TIME FOR OUR REVOLUTION

**THE CHILDREN OF TODAY CANNOT
LOVE OUR TOMORROW
IF THE LEADERS OF TODAY DO NOT.**

GO BLUE!

by Kendra Urdang

"Go Blue!"
roars the
bumper sticker
on the back
of her SUV,
a cell phone covered
by blond hair,
she pulls out of her
Starbuck's parking
space without
glancing in the
side-view mirror.
Horns retaliate,
I sigh.

THIS IS MY HOMETOWN.

NAME
Kendra Urdang

AGE
18

SCHOOL Montclair High
School, Montclair, NJ.

Plans to study English or cultural anthropology in
college & is interested in public health and nursing.

drive by the "ghetto" part of town.
pretend not to see the boarded up windows,
the cops at every corner,
the train tracks where houses should be.
drive by the houses with seven bedrooms,
through the floor-to-ceiling windows, you can see
the indoor swimming pools,
hear the swish of tennis rackets
and **PRETEND** that it all looks like this.

and in the classrooms, the imbalance is subtle,
undercurrents in hallways.
AP classes on the top floor, special ed. in the basement
and although over half the faces in the yearbook
are darker than mine,
on the third floor, everyone looks like me.

SO IT SEEMS GLASS CEILINGS ARE OFTEN CONCRETE.

there goes the Principal again.
"Diversity Our Strength, Unity Our Goal"
pinned to his blazer.
he smiles at the white kids and says "good morning"
as we walk into school.
town newspaper comes to take pictures,
every classroom they are shown is **A MECCA OF MIXED FACES**
Principal smiling widely with hope for the future.
and **THIS** is the place I call home.

soccermoms driving SUVs hold
fundraisers for the football team,
"Go Blue!" plastered on their bumpers,
black men are fine
AS LONG AS THEY'RE TACKLING EACH OTHER,
let's raise some more money!
SAY NOTHING when they fail school
and keep them away from your daughters.
so let's stay quiet, ride this pseudo-underground railroad,
this free ticket to funding from the board of ed.
RACISM IS ONLY OUR PROBLEM
IF IT MAKES THE FRONT PAGE.

although brown
faces fill the hallways,
administrators
don't know their names,
they are just the
free ticket
to funding,
and
THIS
IS
NOT
THEIR
SCHOOL.

27

TELL ME IF THIS MAKES SENSE

by Ariane A. Gilgeous

Tell me if this makes sense
I THINK I MISSED SOMETHING
"The Policy of Separating..."
THERE WAS A POLICY?
A strategy to segregate?
Yeah, there was
and now it has moved from **POLICY** to **NORMALCY**.

It's **NORMAL** now for kids like me
URBAN KIDS
MINORITY KIDS
TO HAVE CRAP FOR BOOKS
And broken down schools.

It's **NORMAL** now
For kids like me
Urban kids
Minority kids
To ask:
WHY ARE MY BOOKS FIVE, TEN, FIFTEEN,
TWENTY YEARS OLDER THAN
THE BOOKS THEY GET IN THE SUBURBS?

NAME Ariane Ashley Gilgeous

AGE 14

SCHOOL Science Skills Center High School, Brooklyn, NY.

Plans to study psychology, theater & music in college.

WHY are so many pages missing from my books?

WHY are my classrooms so crowded?

WHY am I the only Black, Asian, or Latina girl in my AP class?

WHY do our teachers ask us for the answers to the math problems?

WHY are so many of them without proper degrees?

WHY is the paint chipping in my school's hallways?

WHY are there insults and disses carved into my desks,

AND Why am I beginning to do it, too?

This **DOESN'T** make sense!

I KNOW I MISSED SOMETHING!

The last time I checked this was still a problem.

Brown versus the Board of Education says

WE DESERVE THE SAME EDUCATION.

We've lost respect for our schools.

But, I guess we've accepted it,

right?

FOCUS/REFOCUS

by Emily Gena

THAT DOESN'T APPLY TO YOU

Señor Suit con su striped corbata
Your Bandera Americana branded to your lapel
Mademoiselle Mercedes with the child seat
In the back
With Oscar De La Renta skinned chromosomes

YOU ARE MAKING A DIFFERENCE

You don't litter
You made a contribution to (Insert charity here)
Because of the plaque hanging in your home office
The one you remodeled the basement den for
So you could spend more time at home
That would have no justification in
The categorization of your offspring
His genetic makeup would be just fine
At least from what you contributed to the baby making process
But you said so
You said "Some people are genetically less intelligent"

WHOSE GENETICS EXACTLY ARE INFERIOR?

WHOSE GENETICS EXACTLY ARE MISSING A FEW CROSSBARS ON THE DOUBLE HELIX?

WHOSE GENETICS ARE YOU EXAMINING THROUGH YOUR MICROSCOPE?

You don't need to specify

NAME Emily Genao

AGE 18

SCHOOL Fordham University, Bronx, NY.

Studying communications and hopes to become a newspaper or magazine journalist.

Since it is misconceived that those people are usually the ones
With the sun kissed skin
The doorman who suffers through the 2-hour train ride from Queens
The cleaning lady trying to hold down 2 jobs and a newborn at home
The kid who plays his Slipknot CD too loud
YOU WOULDN'T SIT NEXT TO HIM ANYWAY
When you slide my culture under your power magnification you see **ME**:
A first generation college student
Actress who will transcend the role of rape victim, maid, gossiping neighbor
Poet whose grass roots are growing back in again
Dancer with salsa in her hips and azucar in her blood
Dreamer of Puerto Rican sunsets, Manhattan darkness,
with a scar on her Lower East Side
Only it isn't your microscope
It was passed on to you from your ancestral scientists

NOW IT'S YOUR TURN
To look at everyone through the
Antiquated lens
Only you don't turn it on yourself
BECAUSE YOU DIDN'T INHERIT INFERIOR DNA

A CALL TO ACTION

by Yasmine Blanding

Umm...What crowd of people do I want to talk to...

Truthfully I want to call you all out.

I WANT TO CALL EACH AND EVERYONE OF YOU OUT WHO PUT MORE THOUGHT INTO THE PROBLEM THAN THE SOLUTION.

I want to call each and everyone of you out who have a chair in the meetings

that are **SUPPOSED TO MAKE A DIFFERENCE** in our schools, and society.

I want to call all of you out who make call to actions and not make actions we can call on.

I want to tell all the secrets of how you make all your decisions by **WHAT YOU BELIEVE**,

by **WHAT YOU VALUE**, never once taking **YOU** out of the equation.

How at all the wrong reasons you're acting all stout.

Holding the truth, what needs to be shared...

WHAT MY EDUCATIONAL SITUATION IS REALLY ABOUT.

The lack of inventory of books, computers, and most important teachers,

the judgment of more than just my old beat up sneakers...the real issues.

With powerful thoughts, I'm not worried with your faults...

because we are all human.

With controlling eyes, we watch with our lives (we live follow the leader)

With a heart with might, for what's right **YOU'RE NOT PUTTING A FIGHT...**

without your acknowledgement your ideas are taking flight...in the wrong direction and

with words to command **YOU NEVER, YOU NEVER SPEAK UP.**

Denouncing your capacity to exert an influence—

you live beneath yourself, trying to please those that dwell beneath you.

NAME Yasmine Blanding

AGE 21

SCHOOL York College, Jamaica, NY.

Hopes to become a high school guidance counselor after she completes her degree in psychology.

After all those meetings, and all those seatings, all the phone calls,
all the falls. The long lines and paid physical fines.
Through all the research, pain and hurt.
You're going to tell me the time has been worth no more than dirt.

YOU MUST SPEAK UP FOR YOUR WORDS ARE ARRESTED.
YOU MUST SPEAK UP FOR YOUR WORDS ARE CONGESTED.

YOU CANNOT AFFORD TO STOP HERE! You are not giving anymore than you can bear.
You do not have the spirit of fear. **SO THE DOUBTING OF YOUR SELF MUST STOP HERE.**
I'm robbed of my good days out weighing my bad days, and without an input…
You dare to complain this is as serious as people being robbed of departing planes.
YOU'RE ALL OUT OF CHARACTER JUST TO GET FAME, and still you have your sane brain
and still about the wrong issues you complain.
Ah, If I could just share with you how much my generation has in store.
I'm not talking about pushing others to the floor, just to make it.
I'm talking about **CONQUERING SOME MORE, JUST TO MAKE IT…**
To make the way for the future to come, I get angry at your lack of interest
just thinking about when the end result of our lives are finally done.
EVERY MOMENT OF THE DAY WE SHOULD BE WORKING. EACH ONE, **REACHING ONE,**
TEACHING ONE. EACH ONE YOU AND I, REACHING ONE. The old.
The new and the few. Teaching one. Teach about our beauty, our history, and our battle.

WE MUST RISE TO OUR TRUE SELVES.

We have work to do, I encourage you to not die with your work balled up in your fist.
Time is of the Essence.

SPEAK UP AND WHILE FREEING YOUR SELF AND YOUR WORDS…
PROSPERITY WILL THEN BE AMONG MY GENERATION.

THE **BUTTERFLY** EFFECT

by Joanna Robert

ALL THE WORDS WE SAY TODAY
WILL COME BACK TO US ON OUR DOORSTEP
IN THE NEWSPAPER TOMORROW.

Scientists tell us that the world of nature is so small and interdependent
that a butterfly flapping its wings in the Amazon could cause
a violent storm on the other side of the earth.
I have discovered that when a stranger offers to push another stranger
in her wheelchair as she struggles to carry her grocery bags
filled with orange juice and pent up emotions, it could cause
A REVOLUTION OF BLIND GIVING, EVERYWHERE.
It's easy to limit your understanding of yourself to believe that you
are insignificant, that your act of saving a spider on the floor by bringing
it outside on a tissue will have no effect on our infinitely
interconnected world. But, in truth, it could cause a deaf man to choose
to teach sign language after a lifetime of being mainstreamed.

NAME
Joanna Roberts

AGE 18

SCHOOL Mamaroneck High School, Mamaroneck, NY.

Hopes to study languages, law, & international relations & to become a lawyer or journalist.

And when a teacher in my high school,
UNCHALLENGED BY ANY AUTHORITY,
screams at a group of Latino kids outside his classroom that
Food Emporium is looking for help,
THE YOUTH OF AMERICA WILL SHIVER AT FIRST,
but then **WE WILL RISE UP** AND DANCE AND SING OUR PRIDE AND
THROW OUR HANDS UP IN OUR MARCH FOR EQUALITY.
Yesterday I was standing on a street corner in the rain, and I looked
around and noticed that there was a man standing to my right holding
his umbrella over my head. I could faintly hear the children
in Southern Bihar **BURSTING INTO LAUGHTER OVER SUNBEAMS.**
All the words we say today will come back to us on our
doorstep in the newspaper tomorrow.

MATH CLASS

by Iralma Osorio Sorondo

YOU ARE INHERENTLY UN-EQUAL.
That's what you motherfuckers tell me by giving me books
that are 10 years older than Ms. Charlie's Angels over there.
**YEAH YOU, SEÑOR SUIT CON SU STRIPPED CORBATA
AND YOUR BANDERA AMERICANA.**
I inherited in-equality.
Because you put me **IN THE BACK** of Ms. Kramer's class when
we had supervisors scanning the room.
OVERLOOKING BLACK BODIES with books that have stark colors.
They're overwhelmed by pretty blue-eyed faces with shining books and initials
embedded into their hard cover.
**THE SUBWAY TOURIST MAP DOESN'T GO FURTHER THAN 125TH STREET =
I'M NOT HERE.**
440 + X = 540
RESPECT AND EQUALITY.
The two words that mean nothing when the constitution
repeats the respect and equality
but they don't mean shit…
Shit meannnnsss.
Shit man, what the fuck is up with school?
The woman's leadership sign is in the garbage
Yet the boy's ultimate Frisbee team scored high and won the goal yesterday
according to the second period announcements.
Second period.
So that everyone knows.

NAME
Iralma Osorio Sorondo

AGE
17

SCHOOL The Beacon
School, New York, NY.

Plans to study theater in college
& hopes to become an actress.

I AM UN-EQUAL =
My books filled with *Motherfucker*
Bitch
Turn to page 169, *Faggot*
Dicks drawn into Rosa Park's mouth
Find out not only the white folk but the brothers wrote that shit =
Anger x ignorance x just not giving a fuck about your culture.
Ask Cindy if she did that…
Her eyes shutter with ignorance
Reply with a simple "You speak that way, I was brought up better."
Brought up better?

YET **I INHERITED IN-EQUALITY**
Subway tourist maps don't go further than 125th Street =
I'M NOT HERE.
$(AB)2 = AABB$
"Um, excuse me, Kathleen, can I borrow your book, I think someone stole mine?"
"I'm sorry, I can't, you understand." =
"I would, but my father told me not to get Puerto Rican fingerprints on it,
he doesn't want me involved in a crime."

BROUGHT UP BETTER?
Yet I'm the one inheriting in-equality.
$440 + X = $ what?
$(AB)2 = $ who?
Nothing.
This is, in fact, my poker face Mr. Suit con su stripped corbata
and your bandera Americana.

TAKE THAT RED, WHITE AND BLUE OFF AND LOOK AT ME.

NO **YOU**

SHUT UP!

by Annique Roberts

NO YOU SHUT UP!

You—the **MISEDUCATOR** and **MISINFORMER**

You—**THE HISTORY REWRITER THAT TRIES TO CONTAIN MY GENERATION**

to one-sided tongues

YOU SHUT UP BECAUSE I'VE SHUT UP SO LONG MY DOWN IS WIDE OPEN

gaping for voices hungry for words unspoken

YOUR LIES OF MY STORY ARE DEPRESSING TO SIT IN

oozing and surrounding my temple's foundation

that quivers at the very thought of sinking into nothingness

I'D RATHER STAND IN THE TRUTHS OF MY GREAT GRANDS

TIPTOEING ON THEIR SHOULDERS AS I REACH FOR HIGHER GROUNDS

beyond all your textbooks pound into my innocence

YOU BRAINWASH ME WITH GLORIES OF X AND KING

Including Rosa and how her poor feet were aching

But what slipped your mind; what you forgot to mention

is a captain, a king, like Bayard Rustin

Afraid that being gay would retard progression

he held his lifestyle in quiet suppression

to maintain the credit of a Marching Washington

These generals in the fight—their stories weren't different

They all had a dream in the freedom movement

NAME Annique Roberts

AGE 21

SCHOOL Graduated from Howard University in Washington, D.C. in 2004.

Has been accepted into the Garth Fagan Dance company in Rochester, NY.

Ella Baker traveled the South in hopes of creating
Individual communities capable of sustaining
A struggle that had become worldwide
SHIFTING FOCUS TO A HUMAN PRIDE
One filled with **KNOWING THE TRUTH OF OUR PAST**
And enforcing a way of serving that would last
SSSSSSSSSSSHHHHHHHHHH!!!!!!!!!!!!!!!!!!
You see, you tell stories of only individuals, forgetting that they moved
and collaborated with **A MASS OF MANY**

You want us to wait for the resurrection of a dream that never even died

MOVING CIVIL RIGHTS HASN'T ENDED

You just succeeded in telling us that what we needed

Was to hang around waiting for someone to guide us from the fall

I no longer come to you for answers

I **LOWER** MY RAISED HAND AND **RAISE** MY LOWERED HEAD

to educators outside the classroom walls

And now in your silence

WE SEE THE ABILITY TO LEAD THRIVES IN US ALL

…Ahhhhh, now how does it feel to be silent?

SEPARATE EQUALITY

by Malan Bullock

"Separate Equality" has no place in my palm.
Nor my children's children's touch.
Cause I never fathom it before.
But this ignorance is not as blissful, as it seems!
SUDDENLY, RACIALLY INTEGRATED INTO A CATEGORY
Where the **UNKNOWING** and **ACCUSTOMED TO NEVER UNDERSTANDING**
Is similar to my skin and his skin
LIKE MY GRANDFATHER'S SKIN TO MY FUTURE GRANDDAUGHTERS.
From **MAPLE SYRUP** to **CARAMEL** to **MAHOGANY**
BACK TO CINNAMON TOAST LACED WITH BUTTER
But I grew wiser and cleared eyed
Then I die
When I become blind and timeless in statues
A slab will read
"Let separate but equal have no place in my hand.
Only God's power be in my hand
Allow his word to come from my hand and shock you."
Out of the Palm, you will hear
Only King's utterance of letting freedom ring
Pause

'Til it will reach the deepest oceans

Ringing for bleeding ears to hear

CRACKING THE LIBERTY BELL TO MILLIONS OF PIECES

SINCE LIBERTY HAS NOT RUNG IN A LONG TIME.

Ring 'til education and mental development

spill from my cousin's lips

Into the common speech of the world

These words will metamorphose into textbooks of Conquest

OVER THE INHERENTLY UNEQUAL SUPPORTS

TO PUSH DOWN THE DESTINED ONES.

So the bell will ring

And **RING**

AND STILL RING

And **RING...DING**

And **DING**

DING...

DING...

DING...

DING...

CLASSIFICATION

by Amir Bilal Billups

I was walking up the street with my boy Anthony and this other kid.
Anthony was making jokes and the other kid turned around
and asked, **"ARE YOU IN SPECIAL ED?"**
My man said, **"YES."**
Soon after, being in my six person class, like yesterday I remember
South Orange / Maplewood School District **CLASSIFIED ME.**
It was 2000.
She said I was **"ELIGIBLE FOR SPECIAL EDUCATION."**
Possessing this label they gave me,
I SWALLOWED THE STIGMA and **FELT THE PAIN** of being
seen in a room with six people.
Yeah, it fell upon me and the pain was like stones raining down on me.
From the day where school assemblies seemed segregated
and I had to watch my girl Krystal from balconies…
AWAY FROM THE "NORMAL" KIDS to the days where I found myself
fulfilling self-fulfilled prophecies.
See I received **THE LABEL** of "special education"
and it sat on my back like a mountain being lifted by an ant—
it just can't happen.
IT WAS MY MIND'S MASTER.
It told me I was dumb, I didn't know how to act in a normal class.

NAME
Amir Bilal Billups

AGE
17

SCHOOL Columbia High School,
South Orange / Maplewood, NJ.

Plans to study history in college & hopes
to become a high school history teacher.

I needed **TWO** teachers to fully grasp the concepts touched upon in class,
and my classification will never allow me to exceed track two.

SO WHAT IS IT THAT I DO—so many occasions
when the classification caused me to break into tears?

IT WAS MY FRUSTRATION.

My reaction to teachers speaking down to me saying
I was classified and it was all my fault.
Had me truly believing that inferiority was my classification.

CAUSE I STILL DIDN'T KNOW,

and the pain WAS DEEP. The pain—OH GOD! THE PAIN!

THE RIDICULE,

THE CONSTANT TAUNTING,

LAUGHING

WHEN THEY PASSED ME BY.

Told me that community college should be my goal.
It wasn't until Ms. Cooper came and rescued me with her history class.
Showed me **THE IMPORTANCE OF MY HISTORY** and told me
the secrets my ancestors held.
She told me about the Malcolm Xs and the Huey Newtons.

SHE TOLD ME TO SPEAK OUT

BECAUSE THIS IS THE STORY OF MANY AND NONE OF THEM ARE SPEAKING.

And the silence is just as painful.

RAP STAR

by Natasha Alexander

Simply being gifted
Was your limitation
NOT ENCOURAGED to be a doctor or teacher
Made to believe that
Your only true place of success
Is in being some sort of **ENTERTAINER** or **ATHLETE**

Talk in the staff meeting
NOT about **YOUR B+ PAPER**
But about **HOW MANY YARDS**
you can throw a football
OR your **THREE POINT SHOT**
OR your **BEAUTIFUL TENOR VOICE**

You're behind bars now
Upon you those teachers look down
Because they say they put all their time into you
YOUR PATH IS WHAT YOU CHOOSE, RIGHT?
I guess they were never taught that
TEACHERS HAVE A HIGH CALLING

Oh Rap Star, the basement is just cold
No stage lights, hoes and cars
No buying rounds of drinks at bars
Just the silent memories of young men
in this cell before you
Echo from window to door
You can feel it from ceiling to floor
YOU'RE DEAD TO THE CORE
YOU FELT THIS BEFORE

NAME
Natasha Alexander

AGE
16

SCHOOL Urban Academy,
New York, NY.

Plans to study history in college & hopes to
be a college professor or attend law school.

About to be shipped off
Too far from the freedom
You were once used to
The liberty God gave you
The only real privilege you were born into

GONE, gone with the bang of a gavel
In a court room
WHERE JUSTICE, WHO CAN'T SEE
Points arms outstretched to sentence you
TO LIFE, TO REAL LIFE, TO THE REST OF YOUR LIFE
To the life of so many other young men like you
Who share this same fate too.

Oh Rap Stars
YOUNG SHOOTING STARS
OH NOT SO BRIGHT FUTURE STARS
Your heavenly bodies behind bars

So Rap Star spit
Your sorrow to the bars and pavement
While you sit all alone
In a cold sad placement
Waiting for your starship to come.

UNCOMFORTABLE

Natasha Alexander and Elinor Marboe

UNCOMFORTABLE

Kinda like when the bully decides he wants to get violent
So he puts you in a headlock so tight—
That he crushes your larynx, or voice box,
or boxed voice
My windpipe is pulled like a cylinder of chewing gum by dry, ashy fingers,
well into my pelvis.)
Even after he releases
MY NECK IS IN PIECES.
And two lungs, my own, have shrunk to the size of baseballs
where clusters of alveoli bunch together
real tight real tight
REAL TIGHT REAL TIGHT.

The first thing we do is make noise, babies cry
What's life without a shout or a sigh? Shout, laugh, giggle, mumble, sing, sigh
It doesn't feel good to be silent.
But after a while it stops feeling bad
Because you've had to eat it so long
You've become accustomed to the taste
The flavor becomes familiar, like an old friend's face.
It doesn't feel good to be silent
And this Kingdom suffereth violence
And the violent take it be force
God has written my fate.
Oh, silencer you cannot change

My course, but remember and
Understand that silence is a choice.
It doesn't feel good to be silent.
Except for when it does.
Can't I be my own best friend?
To keep my thoughts and doxologies, sometimes
Means more power to me.

Praise God from whom all blessings flow I was given two ears and one tongue

Can't I listen more than I speak?
Praise Him all creatures here below Where is the harm in that?
The 'lent' in silent means I'm
Praise him above ye heavenly host Giving that space back.

To be quiet in public earned me

The title Ice Queen.
Praise Father, Son and Holy Ghost
I'm not frozen.
Nothing is as warm as self.
42% of white American teenagers in public schools
speak up when they hear racist comments.
Bold
Decisive
Be fierce
Be confident
BE HONEST

But what kind of schools do we have where 58%
of white students don't speak out against hatred?

Being quiet is a strong choice—except when it isn't.

ONE HAND CLAPPING

by Elinor Marbo

HOW DO YOU OPEN-FACE SANDWICH SOMEONE?
If meat or cheese can be sandwiched between two pieces of bread,
then two people can "sandwich" a third between them.
But if an open-faced sandwich is meat or cheese with bread on one side,
can you "open-face sandwich" someone?
We know the sound of two hands clapping,
WHAT IS THE SOUND OF ONE HAND CLAPPING?

School shaped like a dumbbell
Barbell, lifting, lifted, pump, pumping.
Veins hunching out of necks, biceps
School shaped like a barbell—
TWO SEPARATE BUILDINGS CONNECTED BY A BAR OF A HALLWAY.

    A-WALL in my school
Means freshmen
Eager nervousness beneath ass-tight jeans
and small bright tee-shirts.
Not the entire freshman class, mind you,
the white, Jewish component.
Dark kids are sparse at A-Wall,
STICK OUT LIKE CHOCOLATE COVERED STRAWBERRIES

NAME
Elinor Marboe

AGE
17

SCHOOL Mamaroneck High School,
Mamaroneck, NY.

Plans to study history and religion
in college.

next to the Juicys.
SELF SEGREGATION in my public high school
Different colored threads, on separate rolled spools.
Is this a topic on which I can speak?
BECAUSE MY SKIN ISN'T BROWN
VERSUS BOARD.

The Hispanic kids who sit in the Post Cafeteria
—do I sit with them?
Well, no.
We get along. We get along well. **ONE HAND.**
ONE HAND OF THE SOLUTION.
But few kids have friends of other races.
Where is that other hand?

There was **ONE** black girl in my AP American class.
One day we read a poem comparing Booker T. to W.E.B.
And we all stared at Alana
waiting for her response.
Then we realized we were staring,
and slowly turned our heads, real casual,
LIKE NOTHING HAD HAPPENED.
BUT IT HAD.

Also to take into account:
White kids unfairly assessed in eighth grade
can never take AP Calculus, AP Bio, AP Chem,
NEED I GO ON?
Tracking isn't bad for minorities.
Tracking is bad.
Tracking is bad.
TRACKING IS LIKE ALL THOSE CHINESE WORKERS
WHO DIED BUILDING THE TRANSCONTINENTAL RAILROAD.
Sure, it seemed like the best method at the time.
Sure, let's group children by abilities in eighth grade.
Tracking is a lot of dead Chinese people somewhere in Nevada.

AND TRACKING ISN'T EVEN OUR BIGGEST ISSUE.

In the commons of my Westchester public high school
sits a girl I was once friends with.
Miraculously, between junior high and the present,
she's developed a South Bronx accent. It's no accident.
Does she remember that time we dressed up as flappers?
I'm not about to ask her.
Not after freshman days of unreturned smiles.
MY SKIN ISN'T BROWN V. BOARD

We know the sound of two hands clapping.
BUT WHAT IS THE SOUND OF ONE HAND CLAPPING?

Kids are taught at my high school that communities are divided by race—
THIS IS THE NORM. THIS IS ACCEPTABLE.
This **BLISTER** of a problem, turning purply red
and filling with fluid as we speak:
My education, my school is shaped like a barbell,
AND I'M ONLY AT ONE END.

RESEARCH FINDINGS

DOCUMENTING THE LEGACY OF BROWN

PARTICIPATORY ACTION RESEARCH FINDINGS

In January of 2002, **The Opportunity Gap Project** was born. With initial support from the Rockefeller Foundation, youth from urban and suburban high schools in New York and New Jersey, joined researchers from the Graduate Center of the City University of New York in a participatory action research collaborative. We worked together to document youth perspectives on educational opportunity gaps across urban—suburban lines, and within racially desegregated suburban high schools. More than 100 high school students participated in a series of research "camps" in which they were immersed in methods training, learning about interviews, focus groups, survey design and participant observation. Together we crafted a youth survey, translated it into Spanish, French-Creole and Braille and distributed it to over 10,000 youth from 15 urban and suburban districts. Focused on questions of distributive and procedural (in)justice in the nation and its schools, the survey includes standard items on attitudes toward school, a cartoon designed to tap relations with educators, a chart depicting the achievement gap and open-ended questions such as, "What is the most powerful thing a teacher has ever said to you?" Between camps, youth conducted research in each others' schools, traversing the urban—suburban fault lines of finance (in)equity, and traveled into each others' classrooms, traversing the 'within-school' fault lines of academic tracks.

Nikaury Acosta, Yelena Allakhverdev, Jacob Bartholemew, Emily Brisbon, Christine Doyle, Emily Genao, Melanie Harris, Candace de Jesus, Antoine McKenzi, Shamaya Mickens, Chris Murphy, Amanda Osorio, Charles Penn, Norman Rahman, Magisel Rivera, Sati Singleton, Anthony Smith, Travis Staten, Shantaine Stevens, Tamir Stevens, Fidel Tavarez, Jordana Viuker, Ashley Webb.

We present here a summary of our findings, sketching the **generational victories of Brown, the ongoing struggles for racial justice in education, and the spaces of intellectual equity** that dot today's educational landscape. For more details on this research, we invite you to scan the references at the back of this volume—read our publications, visit our website, watch our video, dive into our DVD, to learn how youth theorize and respond to the severe imbalance of educational opportunities they witness and experience, 50 years after Brown.

Spanish form (left)

Señale el grado:

9 (10) 11 12

Nombre de la escuela:

_____

SUS OPINIONES
sobre su escuela y sobre Estados Unidos

Nos gustaría saber lo que **usted** piensa sobre su escuela y sobre Estados Unidos.

Un equipo de investigación compuesto por estudiantes de escuelas secundarias en New York y New Jersey (algunos en la foto), junto con un equipo de investigadores del Graduate Center de la Universidad de la Ciudad de New York, están entrevistando alrededor de 7.000 estudiantes de 13 distritos de la ciudad de Nueva York, Nueva Jersey y del estado de Nueva York, para conocer sus opiniones acerca de sus escuelas y sobre nuestro país.

¿Por qué?

Porque tanto los educadores, como los gobernantes, así como los medios de comunicación y otros estudiantes, deben escuchar las opiniones de los **estudiantes**, y no sólo las de los **políticos**.

Esto es un cuestionario, no es un examen.

Su nombre no aparecerá en el cuestionario. No hay ninguna pregunta que pueda relacionar sus respuestas con usted. No hay respuestas correctas o incorrectas, y por tanto, usted no va a obtener una cantidad de puntos al final. Su participación es voluntaria. A pesar de que no está obligado/a a contestar a las preguntas que aparecen a continuación si no quiere, esperamos que lo haga, ya que es importante que la gente empiece a oír lo que piensan los estudiantes.

Opiniones sobre Estados Unidos

1. La gente tiene diferentes opiniones sobre Estados Unidos.
Marque con una cruz la casilla que esté debajo de la frase que mejor refleja su opinión.

	No estoy de acuerdo en absoluto	No estoy de acuerdo	Estoy de acuerdo	Estoy completamente de acuerdo
En general todo el mundo recibe un trato justo en Estados Unidos, independientemente de quiénes sean.	☒	☐	☐	☐
En los Estados Unidos un estudiante de familia de "bajos ingresos económicos" (low income), tiene las mismas posibilidades de recibir una buena educación que un estudiante de familia con dinero.	☐	☐	☒	☐
En Estados Unidos tenemos la capacidad de cambiar de gobierno si no nos gusta lo que hacen.	☐	☐	☒	☐
El racismo ya no es un problema hoy en día en Estados Unidos.	☐	☒	☐	☐
Al gobierno no le interesa lo que piensa la gente como mi familia y como yo.	☐	☐	☒	☐

1

English form (right)

Circle Grade:

(9) 10 11 12

School Name:

_____

YOUR OPINIONS
about the United States and your School

We want to know what **you** think about the United States and your school.

A research team of high school students from New York and New Jersey (some in the photo) and researchers from The Graduate Center of the City University of New York are surveying over 7,000 students from 13 districts in New York City, New Jersey and New York State about your opinions of our country and your schools.

Why?

Because educators, the government, the media and other students need to hear from **students**, not just from **politicians**, about how you feel.

This is a survey, not a test.

Your name is not on the survey. Nothing will connect your answers to you! There are no right or wrong answers and you don't get a score at the end. Your participation is voluntary. Even though you don't have to answer any of the following questions if you don't feel like answering them, we hope you do, because it's important that people begin to listen to what students think.

Opinions about the United States

1. People have different opinions about the United States.
Check the box next to the statement to show how you feel.

	Strongly Disagree	Disagree	Agree	Strongly Agree
Basically people get fair treatment in the United States, no matter who they are.	☐	☐	☑	☐
In the United States, a "low income" student has the same chance of a good education as a "wealthy" student.	☐	☑	☐	☐
We have the ability to change the government if we don't like what it is doing.	☐	☐	☑	☐
Racism is no longer a problem in the United States.	☐	☑	☐	☐
The government doesn't really care what people like my family and I think.	☐	☑	☐	☐

1

The Opportunity Gap Survey was completed by 9,174 youth from 15 urban and suburban districts. The survey was created in English, Spanish, French and Braille, by the Opportunity Gap Project, Michelle Fine, Principal Investigator, The Graduate Center, CUNY, 2002.
Database 1 (N=4474) Database 2 (N= 4700). Of those who indicated race/ethnicity: approximately 8% Asian/Pacific Islander; 15% African American; 17% Latino; 8% Afro-Caribbean and 42% White American. (Data base 2 includes 8% multiracial students)

THE GENERATIONAL VICTORIES OF BROWN

■ Aspirations for college

It is important to recognize that we can declare some important victories about the kinds of aspirations and commitments voiced by the Children of Brown. Today, students across race, ethnic, class and geographic lines share equally high academic aspirations, strong commitments to working against social injustice, and deep appreciation for the project of racial integration.

"I CARE A LOT ABOUT MY GRADES."

91.4% of Asian/Pacific Islander American students

94% of African American students

89.8% of White students

80.8% of multiracial students

79% of Latino students

"GOING TO COLLEGE IS PERSONALLY IMPORTANT TO ME."

93% of White American students

88% of Asian/Pacific Islander American students

87% of African American students

87% of Afro-Caribbean students

82% of Latino students

"The worst possible school experience would be..."

Attending a school with lack of materials or teachers to teach.

Going to school and finding out it's a possibility you can't graduate.

Where students are only judged on their grades and how well they do on tests.

To fail standardized tests, and have no friends.

Despite having uniformly high aspirations, these young women and men voice substantial concern about the racial inequities they witness and the post-secondary hurdles they anticipate. African American and Latino students, in particular, worry about their preparation for and access to higher education.

**"MY SCHOOL HAS PREPARED ME FOR COLLEGE
AS WELL AS ANY OTHER STUDENT IN THE U.S."**

73% of White American students

72% of Asian/Pacific Islander American students

65% of Latino students

59% of African American students

**"MONEY MIGHT BE A PROBLEM
THAT KEEPS ME FROM GOING TO COLLEGE."**

57.4% of Latino students

46.8% of African American students

46.2% of multiracial students

41.7% of Asian/Pacific Islander American students

32% of White students

Ironically,
across school
districts,
the very students
who most
need academic
supports for college,
such as SAT
Prep and Tutors,
are least likely
to enjoy
such access.

**"HAVE YOU PARTICIPATED
IN PSAT/SAT PREP COURSES?"***

66% of White American Seniors

61% of Asian American Seniors

47% of African American Seniors

46% of Latino Seniors

45% of Afro-Caribbean Seniors

*73% of high track White American Seniors compared with 39% of low track African American Seniors have participated in PSAT/SAT Prep across districts.

■ Engaged citizenship

Virtually all students voice concerns
about racism, and many feel alienated from
the government in this country:

"Racism is no longer a problem in the U.S."
92% disagree or strongly disagree

**"The government doesn't really care what
people like my family and I think."**
47% agree or strongly agree

Most of the children of Brown express strong commitments to movements for social justice.

**PERCENTAGE OF YOUTH WHO RATE THE
FOLLOWING GOALS AS "VERY IMPORTANT TO ME"**

"Helping those less fortunate than I am"	**84%**
"Ending racism"	**81%**
"Improving my community"	**77%**
"Protecting the environment"	**75%**
"Changing how this country is run"	**42%**

**"IF I HEAR SOMETHING THAT IS RACIST OR
OFFENSIVE TO A GROUP OF PEOPLE I USUALLY
SPEAK UP ABOUT IT."**

67% of African American students

58% of Latino students

55% of Asian/Pacific Islander American students

54% of multiracial students

42% of White American students

White American students
are significantly less likely
to express such
commitments in public.

■ Belief in the project of racial integration

Students express substantial support for integration in their schools:

"ATTENDING A RACIALLY INTEGRATED SCHOOL IS VERY IMPORTANT TO ME"

79% of Asian/Pacific Islander American students

77% of African American students

75% of Latino students

74% of White American students

These same students are quite concerned about inequities in their schools.

"MY SCHOOL IS NOT AS GOOD AS IT SHOULD BE IN PROVIDING EQUAL OPPORTUNITY FOR STUDENTS OF COLOR."

41% of African American students

40% of Afro Caribbean students

30% of Latino students

23% of Asian/Pacific Islander American students

20% of White American students

"The best possible school experience for me would be…"

Engaging, diverse classes in which teachers are concerned with equal representation of all races and orientations, genders in history and literature.

A school system where there is no favoritism because of sex/race. An equal opportunity for all students and rules which are fair and considerate of the students.

To be able to have honors classes and have teachers see through the color of my skin.

A school where I learn as much about Blacks as I do Whites.

Where all my classes aren't Black students like myself because it's level 2 or 3.

"I think a lesbian or gay student would feel comfortable and equal in my school."
56% of all students **disagree** or **strongly disagree**

ONGOING SITES OF STRUGGLE
Six Degrees of Segregation

While it is true that there is much to honor 50 years after the Brown v. Board of Education decision, the educational experiences offered by our nation's schools remain profoundly separate and unequal. The legacy of Brown must be assessed not simply in terms of the degree to which bodies of different colors mingle in the same building, but, more boldly, by the extent to which the larger project of racial justice in education has been realized. The struggle for integration was never merely a fight for access. As the elders tell us so eloquently, Brown was also a struggle for citizenship, democracy and collective social justice. In that spirit, the continued and relentless segregation of resources, opportunities and respect assures a denial of equal access, undermines meaningful claims to full citizenship and threatens the fabric of our diverse democracy. Our research, conducted across some of the wealthiest and poorest schools in the nation, confirms what others have found: a series of well established policies and practices assure and deepen the gap. The more separate America's schools are racially and economically, the more stratified they become in achievement.

Whether we consider urban/suburban finance inequity, the systematic dismantling of desegregation, the racially coded academic tracking that organizes most desegregated schools, students' differential experiences of respect and supports in schools, the class, race and ethnicity based consequences of high stakes testing, or the remarkably disparate patterns of suspensions and disciplinary actions, we witness today the structuring and cementing of social inequity across schools and within them. These policies and practices saturate the souls of youth. They represent a slap at Brown then, and a threat to democracy now. We identify below some of these policy veins of segregation—the very policies and practices that have come to be seen as natural in 2004—the ones that produce and secure the racialized denial of educational opportunity.

■ Finance inequities
A continuing struggle in the nation and in New York State

"New York City schools are deficient in instrumentalities of learning.... There are certainly city schools where the inadequacy is not 'gross and glaring.' Some of these schools may even be excellent. But tens of thousands of students are placed in overcrowded classrooms, taught by unqualified teachers, and provided with inadequate facilities and equipment. The number of children in these straits is large enough to represent a systemic failure."

(Excerpt from the June 26, 2003 4-1 ruling in which the Court of Appeals found that New York City's school system is providing an inadequate education to students, Judge Judith Kaye for the majority).

■ A national retreat from desegregation, resulting in more youth attending racially isolated schools

"A half-century after the Supreme Court found that segregated schools are "inherently unequal," there is growing evidence that the Court was correct. Desegregated schools offer tangible advantages for students of each racial group. Our new work, however, shows that U.S. schools are becoming more segregated in all regions for both African American and Latino students. We are celebrating a victory over segregation at a time when schools across the nation are becoming increasingly segregated."

(Orfield and Lee, 2004, Brown at 50: King's Dream or Plessy's Nightmare?
Harvard University Civil Rights Project)

■ Respect and support

Across our investigation of the 13 desegregated suburban school districts, African American and Latino students report significantly greater concerns about low expectations from educators, more frequent experiences of disrespect and alienation, and substantially less access to academic opportunity and supports for college than their White and Asian/Pacific Islander American peers.

"A teacher once told me..."

Not to worry about my grades because I probably won't go to college anyway.

I did very well on my SATs, for a Latina.

That I was the smartest in the class.

That I was going to fail the Regents test.

That I had tremendous potential—you just can't find it yet.

That I should go to college and take art because I am really talented.

Not to ask questions!

That I wasn't smart.

Every one has the ability to be an A student.

That I wouldn't be able to handle an AP math course.

That my class is stupid, all of us.

You're different from other Black students, careful who you hang out with.

"MY TEACHERS THINK I SHOULD BE IN HONORS CLASSES."

68% of Asian/Pacific Islander American students

67% of White American students

53% of Latino students

46% of multiracial students

42% of African American students

"A STUDENT'S RACE/ETHNICITY AFFECTS HOW SOME TEACHERS TREAT THEM."

48% of African American students

47% of multi-racial students

34% of White American students

33% of Latino students

32% of Asian/Pacific Islander American students

"TEACHERS CARE ABOUT STUDENTS LIKE ME."

60% of White American students

46% of Asian/Pacific Islander American students

45% of Latino students

44% of African American students

■ Tracking within schools

In desegregated suburban schools, we found consistently that students enjoy markedly different access to "rigorous curriculum" (AP/Honors classes) by race/ethnicity.

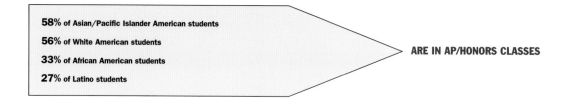

58% of Asian/Pacific Islander American students

56% of White American students

33% of African American students

27% of Latino students

ARE IN AP/HONORS CLASSES

This pattern persists **EVEN FOR THOSE YOUTH WITH COLLEGE-EDUCATED PARENTS.**

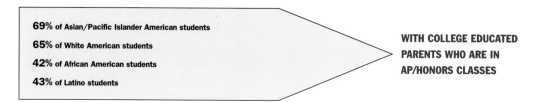

69% of Asian/Pacific Islander American students

65% of White American students

42% of African American students

43% of Latino students

WITH COLLEGE EDUCATED PARENTS WHO ARE IN AP/HONORS CLASSES

While we make no claims that AP/Honors classes are inherently rigorous, they do signify college-bound curriculum and often are taught by the most experienced faculty.

Even for those youth with college educated parents, a substantial opportunity gap remains.

Students express discomfort with this educational imbalance:

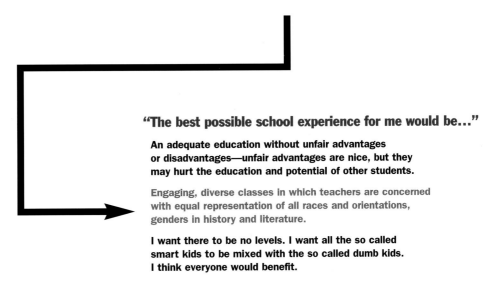

"The best possible school experience for me would be…"

An adequate education without unfair advantages
or disadvantages—unfair advantages are nice, but they
may hurt the education and potential of other students.

Engaging, diverse classes in which teachers are concerned
with equal representation of all races and orientations,
genders in history and literature.

I want there to be no levels. I want all the so called
smart kids to be mixed with the so called dumb kids.
I think everyone would benefit.

**"I WOULD LIKE TO BE IN HIGHER LEVEL CLASSES,
BUT I'M AFRAID THAT I COULDN'T DO THE WORK."**

51% of African American students

50% of Latino students

41% of Asian/Pacific Islander American students

34% of White American students

■ Disciplinary actions and suspension rates

Our data confirm what others have found: that youth of color are disproportionately disciplined, suspended and expelled in desegregated schools.

> **"I HAVE BEEN SUSPENDED IN THE LAST YEAR."**
>
> **23%** of African American students
>
> **19%** of Afro-Caribbean students
>
> **18%** of Latino students
>
> **13%** of Asian/Pacific Islander American students
>
> **10%** of White American students
> reported being suspended

■ High stakes testing, discharge and dropout rates

As many have documented, with the proliferation of high stakes testing such as the Regents requirements in New York State, we are witnessing a dramatic rise in dropout and discharge rates throughout urban communities, particularly for African American and Latino students. Students are explicit about the adverse consequences of these tests, with anxiety and criticism significantly more likely to be expressed by African American and Latino students.

> **"I WORRY THAT STANDARDIZED TESTS CAN PREVENT ME FROM GRADUATING."**
>
> **47%** of Latino students
>
> **44%** of African American students
>
> **33%** of Asian/Pacific Islander American students
>
> **28%** of White American students

On every indicator of the "gap" that we surveyed, African American and Latino students report significantly

SITES OF EDUCATIONAL JUSTICE

Despite the consistent lines of inequity we found etched into urban—suburban borders, and cemented by tracks within suburban communities, we documented a number of spaces in schools, urban and suburban, where young people, from across zip codes, and across racial and ethnic groups, were treated with dignity, engaged in serious academic work, and enjoyed the supports that more privileged families routinely purchase for their children. In particular, on every measure of academic engagement, intellectual challenge and social commitment, urban students in small, performance assessment urban schools—poor, working and middle class; African American, Afro-Caribbean, European American, Latino, Asian and Pacific Islander—rate themselves as highly engaged, challenged and motivated.

Percentage who agree or strongly agree	Large Suburban Schools	Small Urban Schools
Teachers are responsive to students like me.	62%	80%
Teacher know and understand me.	35%	60%
Teachers give me a second chance.	46%	72%
I feel academically challenged.	63%	76%

Despite severe finance inequities, these small urban schools manage to beat the odds in terms of academic engagement and achievement, persistence, graduation and pursuit of higher education for poor and working class youth. The long arm and embrace of Brown can be felt powerfully in these schools, and in a number of classrooms within suburban America. But the full dream is far from realized.

The youth researchers and performers, and the elders who generously narrated their histories, ask for nothing less than racial justice *throughout* the educational system. They are prepared to sacrifice and continue the struggle, knowing now that they are not alone, knowing that they toil in a long and distinguished line of men and women who dare to speak. And today they ask, simply, where you stand, now that the victories, the betrayal and the evidence are so clear.

—*April Burns, Michelle Fine and María Elena Torre, The CUNY Graduate Center*

SOCIAL SCIENCE, SOCIAL JUSTICE AND THE ARTS: THE MANY ECHOES

An extensive collective of high school students, working with university researchers, has labored together over the past two years in the Opportunity Gap Research Project, documenting and analyzing educational (in)justice in varied corners of the U.S. Rooted within this scholarship, the many Echoes— the spoken word/dance performance, video, DVD, publications and the book —have been crafted in a thick multi-generational stew of social theory, social research and the history of social movements. Throughout our collaborations, we have been supported graciously by educators and students' families. With far too many people to acknowledge, we must thank Fred Frelow and Andre Oliver of the Rockefeller Foundation, Cyn Savo of Cynergy, Sherry King, Superintendent of the Mamaroneck Public Schools and director of the Regional Minority Achievement Consortium, Bernadette Anand of Bank Street College, Sara Mastellone and Roberto Reyes of Columbia High School in South Orange/Maplewood, David Surrey of Saint Peter's College, Mark Federman and his colleagues from East Side Community High School and Stan Karp of John F. Kennedy High School in Paterson, New Jersey for their deep commitments to the youth and to sustaining movements for educational justice.

Below, we present the Opportunity Gap Research publications, drawn from schools and communities throughout the metropolitan New York City region, and we credit our amazing colleagues who produced the Summer Institute, video, DVD, book and the performance. These are the creative minds that have lengthened the arc of Brown, joining research, activism and performance in the ongoing struggle for social justice. We are more than indebted.

—Michelle Fine
Distinguished Professor of Psychology,
The CUNY Graduate Center

—María Elena Torre
Research Director, doctoral candidate,
The CUNY Graduate Center

PARTICIPATORY RESEARCH: A GROWING SET OF REFERENCES

Acosta, N., Castillo, J., DeJesus, C., Genao, E., Jones, M., Kellman, S., Osorio, A., Rahman, N., Sheard, L., Taylor, J. with help from Bloom, J. and Chajet, L. (2003). Urban Students Tackle Research on Inequality: What You Thought We Didn't Know. *Rethinking Schools*. 18, No. 1, Fall, 31–32.

Anand, B., Fine, M., Perkins, T., Surrey, D. and the Renaissance School Graduating Class of 2000. (2002). *Keeping the Struggle Alive: Studying Desegregation in Our Town*. New York: Teachers College Press.

Bloom, J. (2004). The hollowed promise of higher education. In Weis, L. and Fine, M. *Beyond Silenced Voices*. Albany: SUNY Press.

Burns, A. (2004). The Racing of Capability and Culpability in Desegregated Schools: Discourses of Merit and Responsibility. In M. Fine, Weis, L., Pruitt, L. and Burns, A. (Eds.), *Off White: Readings on Power, Privilege and Resistance*. New York: Routledge Publishers.

Burns, A. and Torre, M. E. (2004). Shifting Desires: Discourses of Accountability in Abstinence—only Education in the United States. In A. Harris, (Ed.), *All About the Girl: Power, Culture and Identity*. New York: Routledge Publishers.

Fine, M. (2003). *Testimony to the Joint Hearing with the Senate Education Committee. Regents Learning Standards and High School Graduation Requirements*. Albany, New York.

Fine, M., Bloom, J. and Chajet, L. (2003). Betrayal: Accountability from the Bottom. *Voices in Urban Education: Rethinking Accountability*. Providence, RI: Annenberg Institute for School Reform at Brown University. Spring, 2003. http://www.annenberginstitute.org/VUE/spring03/Fine.html

Fine, M., Bloom, J., Burns, A., Chajet, L., Guishard, M. and Torre, M.E. Dear Zora: A letter to Zora Neale Hurston fifty years after Brown. (2004). In Weis, L. and Fine, M. *Working Method*. New York: Routledge Publishers.

Fine, M. and Burns, A. (2003). Class Notes: Toward a Critical Psychology Of Class and Schooling. *Journal of Social Issues*, 59(4), 841–860.

Fine, M., Burns, A., Payne, Y. A. and Torre, M. E. (2004). Civic Lessons: The Color of Class and Betrayal. *Teachers College Record*.

Fine, M., Burns, A. and Torre, M.E. (2004). Postcards from America. In C. Glickman (Ed.) *Letters to the next president: What we can do about the real crisis in public education*. New York: Teachers College Press, 211–222.

Fine, M., Freudenberg, N., Payne, Y. A., Perkins, T., Smith, K. and Wanzer, K. (2003). "Anything Can Happen with Police Around": Urban Youth Evaluate Strategies of Surveillance in Public Places. *Journal of Social Issues*, 59 (1), 141–158.

Fine, M. and Torre, M.E. (2004). Re-membering Exclusions: Participatory action research in public institutions. *Qualitative Research in Psychology*, 1, 1, 15–38.

Fine, M., Torre, M.E., Boudin, K., Bowen, I., Clark, J., Hylton, D., Martinez, M., "Missy," Rivera, M., Roberts, R.A., Smart, P. and Upegui, D. (2003). Participatory action research: Within and beyond bars. In Camic, P., Rhodes, J.E., & Yardley, L. (Eds.), *Qualitative research in psychology: Expanding perspectives in methodology and design*. Washington, DC: American Psychological Association, 173–198.

Fine, M., Torre, M.E., Boudin, K., Bowen, I., Clark, J. Hylton, D., Martinez, M., Missy, Roberts, R.A, Smart, P. and Upegui, D. (2001). *Changing Minds: The impact of college in a maximum security prison*. www.changingminds.ws.

Fine, M., Weis, L., Pruitt, L. and Burns, A. (Eds.). (2004). *Off White: Readings on Power, Privilege and Resistance*. New York: Routledge Publishers.

Genoa, E. (2002). Money for nothing. *The Brooklyn Rail*. http://www.thebrooklynrail.org/ poetry/fall02/money-fornothing.html

Guishard, M., Fine, M., Doyle, C., Jackson, J., Staten, S., and Webb, A. (2004). The Bronx on the move: Activist research by youth as organizing. *The Journal of Educational and Psychological Consultation*.

Guishard, M., Fine, M., Doyle, C., Jackson, J., Roberts, R., Staten, S., Singleton, S. and Webb, A. (May 2003). "As long as I got breath, I'll fight": Participatory action research for Educational justice. *The Family Involvement Network of Educators*. Harvard Family Research Project. http://www.gse.harvard.edu/hfrp/projects/fine.html

Payne, Y. A. (2001). Black men and Street Life as a Site of Resiliency: A Counter Story for Black Scholars. *International Journal of Critical Psychology*. 4, 109–122.

Payne, Y. A. and Brown, A. (2004). Sites of Resiliency: A Reconceptualization of Resiliency for Young Black Men Living in the Ghetto. In M. Pierre (Ed.), *A New Psychology for African-American Men*. Westport, Ct.: Information Age.

Torre, M.E. (2004). The alchemy of integrated spaces: Youth participation in research collectives of difference. In L. Weis and M. Fine (Eds.). *Beyond Silenced Voices*. New York: SUNY Albany Press.

Torre, M.E. and Fine, M. (2004). Bar none: Extending affirmative action to higher education in prison. *Journal of Social Issues*.

Torre, M.E. and Fine, M. (2004) Activism, (out)rage and (in)justice: Participatory action research with youth on the politics of public schools. In L. Sherrod and C. Flanagan (Eds.). *Encyclopedia of youth activism*. Westport, Ct.: Greenwood Publishing Group.

Torre, M.E. and Fine, M. (2003). Youth researchers Critically reframe questions of educational justice. *Evaluation Exchange*. http://www.gse.harvard.edu/ ~hfrp/eval/issue22/pp2.html

Torre, M.E., Fine, M., Boudin, K., Bowen, I., Clark, J., Hylton, D., Martinez, M., Missy, Roberts, R.A., Rivera, M., Smart, P., and Upegui, D. (2001). A space for co-constructing counter stories under surveillance. *International Journal of Critical Psychology*, 4, 149–166.

Weis, L. and Fine, M. (2004). *Beyond Silenced Voices*. New York: SUNY Albany Press.

Weis, L. and Fine, M. (2004). *Working Method: Social (in)justice and Social Research*. New York: Routledge Publishers.

THE OPPORTUNITY GAP RESEARCHERS

**FROM THE CUNY GRADUATE CENTER,
CENTER FOR HUMAN ENVIRONMENTS:**

Michelle Fine, Principal Investigator

María Elena Torre, Project Director

Jennifer Ayala, Janice Bloom, April Burns,
Lori Chajet, Mark Dunetz, Monique Guishard,
James O'Brien, Yasser Arafat Payne,
Tiffany Munn-Perkins and Kersha Smith.

**From Urban and Suburban
High Schools and Communities:**

**Columbia High School
Maplewood, New Jersey:**
Esther Akutekha, Yelena Allakhverdev,
Fabienne Aubourg, Jacob Bartholemew,
Amir Bilal Billups, Emily Brisbon, Melanie Harris,
Charles Penn, Kareem Sergent, Desmonae Perry.

**East Side Community High School
New York, New York:**
Nikaury Acosta, Jasmine Castillo,
Candice DeJesus, Emily Genao, Monica Jones,
Seekqumarie Kellman, Luis Murillo,
Amanda Osorio, Noman Rahman,
Lisa Sheard, Jeremy Taylor.

**Fox Lane High School
Bedford, New York:**
Nicole Artis, Phil Bryd, Jeanne Clark,
Nicole Lopez, Sekina Robinson.

**John F. Kennedy High School
Paterson, New Jersey:**
Tarrick Ahmad, Antoine McKenzie,
Shamaya Mickens, Chris Murphy,
Reinauris Paulino, Magisel Rivera,
Mohammed Romadan, Anthony Smith
Shantaine Stevens, Tamir Stevens.

**Mamaroneck High School
Mamaroneck, New York:**
Rachel Cecil, Jordana Viuker.

**Mothers On the Move
Bronx, New York:**
Christine Doyle, Jeunesse Jackson,
Sati Singleton, Travis Staten, Ashley Webb.

**El Puente Academy for Peace and Justice
Brooklyn, New York:**
Fidel Tavarez, Murillo Tendilla.

**Urban Academy
New York, New York:**
Adam Feeney, Alexis Jones, Joanna Kocub,
Vance Rawles.

**White Plains High School
White Plains, New York:**
Jackie Halas, Maria Soto,
Peter John Viamonte, Kevin Young.

THE ART & SOCIAL JUSTICE INSTITUTE: FROM RESEARCH TO PERFORMANCE

Presenters

Robert Perry
Director of African American Studies Program
Saint Peter's College, New Jersey

James T. Campbell
Associate Professor of American Civilization
Africana Studies and History
Brown University, Rhode Island

Tiffany Joseph
Undergraduate Brown University, Rhode Island

Carol E. Tracy
Executive Director, Women's Law Project
Philadelphia, Pennsylvania

Clare Tracy-Stickney
Acting Assistant Principal, University City High School
Philadelphia, Pennsylvania

Lisette Nieves
Co-Founder ATREVETE!

Marinieves Alba
Hip Hop LEADS Latino Youth Inc.

Patricia J. Williams
James L. Dohr Professor of Law,
Columbia Law School, New York

Support

Christina Glover, Bridget Lopez,
Marty McConnell, Dean Mejia, Edward Thompson, Jason Van Ora
Kimberly Warner-Cohen, Sarah Zeller-Berkman

VIDEO DVD PRODUCTION

Hancock Productions, LLC
Markie Hancock, Director
Kathryn Gregorio, Producer

Camera	Editor
Markie Hancock	Markie Hancock
Mark Ledzian	
	Sound
Original Score	Kathryn Gregorio
Bill Lee	
	Writer
Lighting	Ansley T. Erickson
Joel Burton	
Jackson Lynch	**Interviewer**
	Edward Thompson

DVD AUTHORING

Brooklyn Films
Michael Helman

DVD GRAPHIC DESIGN

Yolanda Cuomo Design, NYC
Associate Designer
Astrid Lewis-Reedy

BOOK DESIGN

Yolanda Cuomo Design, NYC

Associate Designer

Kristi Norgaard

Photography

Neil Selkirk

Premiere of

Echoes of Brown: A Spoken Word, Dance, and Video Performance

At John Jay College Theater, May 15, 2004

VISION
History Stands Still For No One

JOURNEY
Silence and Resounding Voices

DREAM
Casting Shadows and Echoes Forward

....

Artistic Director
Rosemarie A. Roberts

Choreographer and Associate Artistic Director
Ronald K. Brown

Spoken Word with the guidance of URBAN WORD NYC
Jen Weiss, Director

Roger Bonair-Agard

Celena Glenn

Cast	Council of Elders Includes:
Ronald K. Brown	Roscoe Brown, Jr.
Natasha Alexander	Adam Green
Amir Billups	Bailey Jackson
Yasmine Blanding	Theodora Jackson
Malan Bullock	Arthur Kinoy (1920–2003)
Emily Genao	Esther Lee
Ariane Ashley Gilgeous	Sonia Sanchez
Juel Lane	Judge Jack Weinstein
Elinor Marboe	
Annique Roberts	**Costume Designer**
Joanna Roberts	Wunmi Olaiya
Tahani Salah	
Iralma Osorio Sorondo	**Lighting Designer**
Keon C. Thoulouis	Brenda Dolan
Kendra Urdang	

Elders' Video Producer and Director
Hancock Productions, LLC

Stage Manager
Celeste A-Re

Set by
Erik Johnson

Producer
Michelle Fine

The recording of this performance will be available to the public for viewing at the Jerome Robbins Dance Division, The New York Public Library for the Performing Arts at Lincoln Center.

NOTE FROM THE ARTISTIC DIRECTOR

Echoes of Brown is a performance of celebration and protest. As a project blending research, history and art, it is located–like the Brown v. Board of Education decision itself–deep in the space between vision and journey. Witness the youth rise up in their words and bodies to lead us with their energetic, blazing and thundering spirits, and hear our ancestors and council of elders guide us toward the stillness, whispering "listen, listen, listen..."

Understood within Black and Latino cultural frames where words are a call to action, our lives are *testimonios* and witnessing and representing are critical. With love in our hearts, Ronald K. Brown, Jen Weiss, the mentors from Urban Word NYC, and I, as well as many others, saw that the work was to guide the youth to rely on their bodies and souls in the telling of this complicated story that was exhumed from poems, research, academic studies and history. And all the time we were asking ourselves *what history, whose history—whose story* is being told? Was it one story or many stories? And if it was many stories, how were we to tell them without losing specificity or a sense of collective? Refusing to be silent, needing to tell the whole story, the violence story, the anger story, the hope story, the determination story and the victory story, we knew that we had to create a sacred space for all of these experiences to be revealed. From the youth walking backwards in time to remember the history and respond to the memories evoked by the research material; to the council of elders bearing witness and reminding us of their struggles and triumphs; to the ancestors, held in the empty chair—all those unnamed and ordinary people who have struggled for democracy and education who inspire us to take responsibility for our present and future—we created a performance of revelation, celebration and protest.

Echoes of Brown is dedicated to all of those who have daily whispered in our ears their teachings about freedom and justice, who breathed these teachings into our dreams and guided us to make them a reality in this piece. The youth performers will grow larger than life before your eyes in this performance, risking everything and leaving nothing to chance as they embody the echoes of Brown. We hope you are undone and redone by this piece, gather wisdom and strength from it, and, most important, are inspired by it to take action to achieve the quality of public education that is needed in your local communities and beyond.

This powerful ten-month process of listening, witnessing and creating has forever changed my life. I humbly thank the youth and the elders for their dedication to the vision, the journey and the quest to give shape to the dream that has brought us here today.

—Rosemarie A. Roberts

We are deeply grateful to all who contributed to the Research, Institutes and Performances. We would like to acknowledge the support of President Frances Degen Horowitz, Anne Kuite, David Levine, David Manning, Gayle Monahan, Stan Miller and all of the security officers at The CUNY Graduate Center, as well as Robert Watts. The many products of Echoes were made possible through generous support from The Rockefeller Foundation, The Open Society Institute, The Spencer Foundation, The Leslie Glass Foundation and The Edwin Gould Foundation.

Distributed by Teachers College Press,
1234 Amsterdam Avenue, New York, NY 10027
www.tcpress.com

ISBN 0-8077-4497-2

Manufactured in China

11 10 09 08 07 06 05 04
8 7 6 5 4 3 2 1